FANTASTIC
ALPHABETS

BOOKKING
international

CONTENTS

INTRODUCTION

Flowing out of the Lake of Geneva, the Rhone encounters the long wall of the Jura which thrusts it back into Savoy until it reaches Lake Bourget. There, finding an outlet, it rushes into France. In two leaps it has reached Lyons.

In the distance, down the harsh flanks of the Jura, the yellow beds of dried-up torrents sketched out the lines of letter Y.

Have you noticed how picturesque the letter Y is, what countless significances it has? - The tree is a Y; the junction of two roads is a Y; the confluence of two rivers is a Y; the head of

Giuseppe Mitelli. Dream alphabet, copy for drawing, Bologna, 1683.

7

a donkey or of a bullock is a Y; a glass on its stem is a Y; a lily on its stalk is a Y; a supplicant raising his arms to heaven is a Y. This observation may, moreover, be extended to everything that in an elementary fashion constitutes human writing. All that exists in demotic language has been brought there by hieratic language. Hieroglyphs are the essential root of written characters. All letters existed first as signs, and all signs existed first as images.

Human society, the world, man as a whole, are all to be found in the alphabet. Masonry, astronomy, philosophy and all the sciences have here their point of departure, imperceptible but real; and that is as it should be. The alphabet is a source. A is the roof, the gable with its cross-beams, the arch, *arx*; or it is the greeting of two friends, who embrace and shake hands; D is the back; B is the D on the D, the back on the back, the hump; C is the crescent, the moon; E is the subfoundation, the jamb, the console, the architrave, architecture from floor to ceiling in one letter; F is the gallows, the fork, *furca*; G is the horn; H is the facade of the building with its two towers; I is the war-machine launching its projectile; J is the ploughshare, and the horn of plenty; K is the angle of reflection equal to the angle of incidence, one of the keys to geometry; L is the leg with its foot; M is the mountain, or the encampment with its tents side by side; N is the door barred by its diagonal; O is the sun; P is the porter standing with his load on his back; Q is the rump with its tail; R is rest, the porter leaning on his stick; S is the serpent; T is the hammer; U is the urn; V is the vase (from which comes the common confusion between them); I have just said what Y is; X is the crossed swords, the combat, who will be victor? we know not; those of a hermetic nature have thus taken X for the sign of destiny, and algebraists see in it the sign of the unknown; Z is lightning, Z is God.

First, therefore, the house of man and its architecture, then the body of man with its structure and its deformities; then justice, music, the church; war, the harvest, geometry; the mountain, the nomadic life, the cloistered life; astronomy; work and rest; the horse and the serpent; the hammer and the urn, which we over-turn and pair up to make the bell; the trees, the rivers, the roads;

Giuseppe Mitelli. Dream alphabet, copy for drawing, Bologna, 1683.

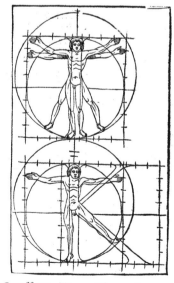

Geoffroy Tory. Champfleury auquel est contenu l'art et la science de la deue et vraye proportion des lettres selon le corps et le visage humain, Paris, 1520.

and lastly, destiny and God; that is what the alphabet holds. Thus it might be that, for some of those mysterious constructors of language who built the foundations of human memory but which human memory has forgotten, the A, the E, the F, the H, the I, the K, the L, the M, the N, the T, the V, the Y, the X, and the Z were no more than the ribs of the framework of the temple.

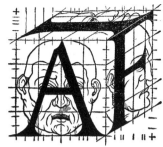

Geoffroy Tory. Champfleury auquel est contenu l'art et la science de la deue et vraye proportion des lettres selon le corps et le visage humain, Paris, 1520.

(Victor Hugo. France et Belgique. Alpes et Pyrénées. Voyages et excursions.)

GROTESQUES

I gallop down the corridors of the labyrinth, I soar over the mountains, I skim the waves, I yelp from the depths of precipices, I cling by my teeth to swirls of storm cloud; with my trailing tail I score the beaches, the hills have modelled their curves on the shape of my shoulders. But you, I find perpetually motionless or, with the point of your claw, drawing alphabets in the sand.

(Gustave Flaubert. La tentation de Saint Antoine.)

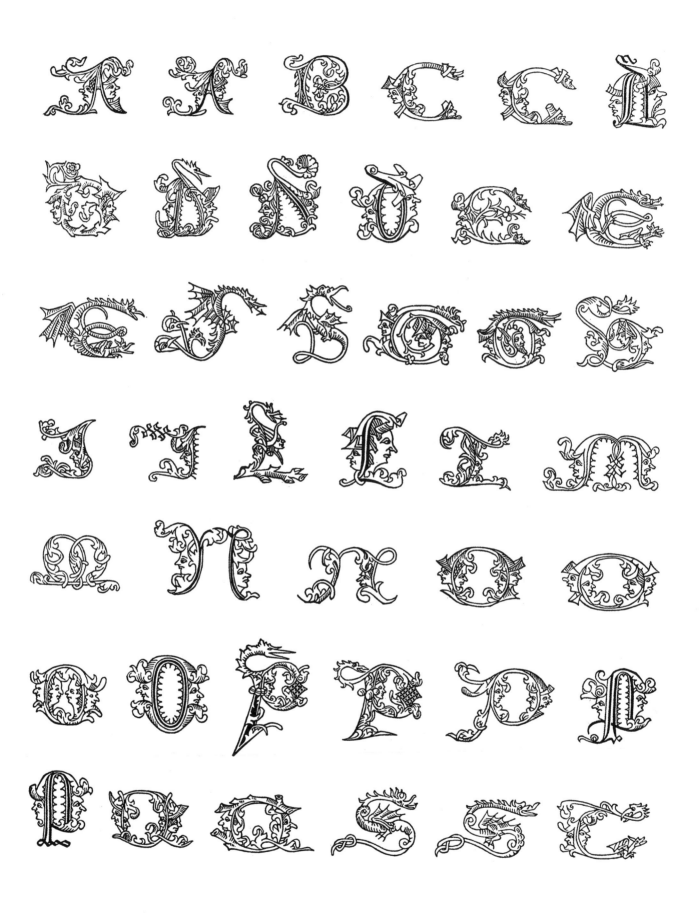

Ornamental capitals. Lyonese school, fifteenth century.

La mer des hystoires

Workshop of Pierre le Rouge. La mer des hystoires,
large decorated initial of the title, Paris, 1488.

13

Ornamental capitals, France, fifteenth century.

Jean de Vingle. La légende dorée, Paris, end of the fifteenth century.

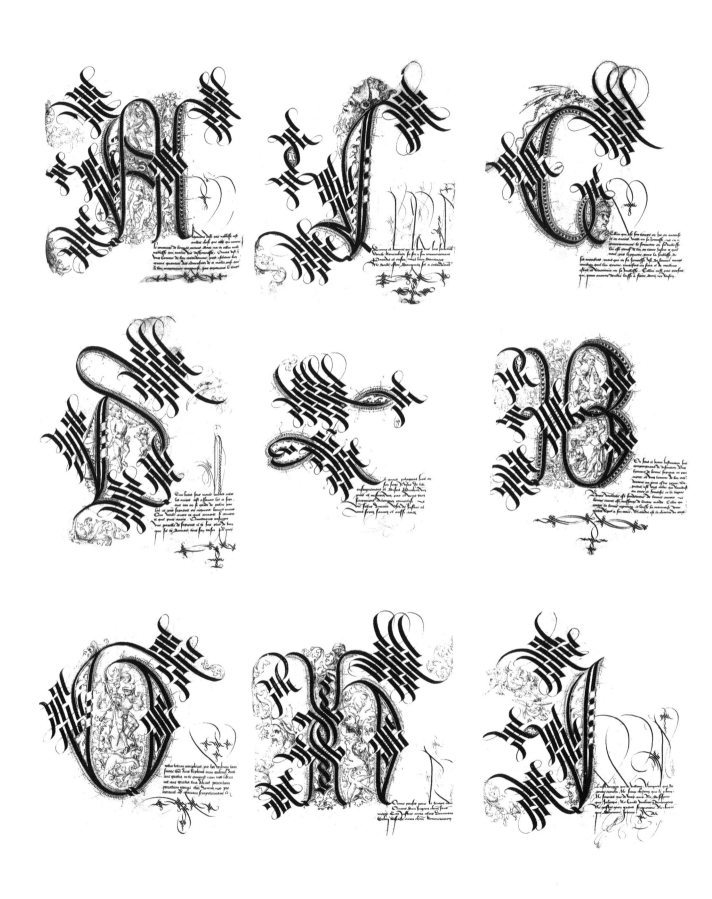

Gothic alphabet of Marie de Bourgogne, circa 1480.

16

Gothic alphabet of Marie de Bourgogne, circa 1480.

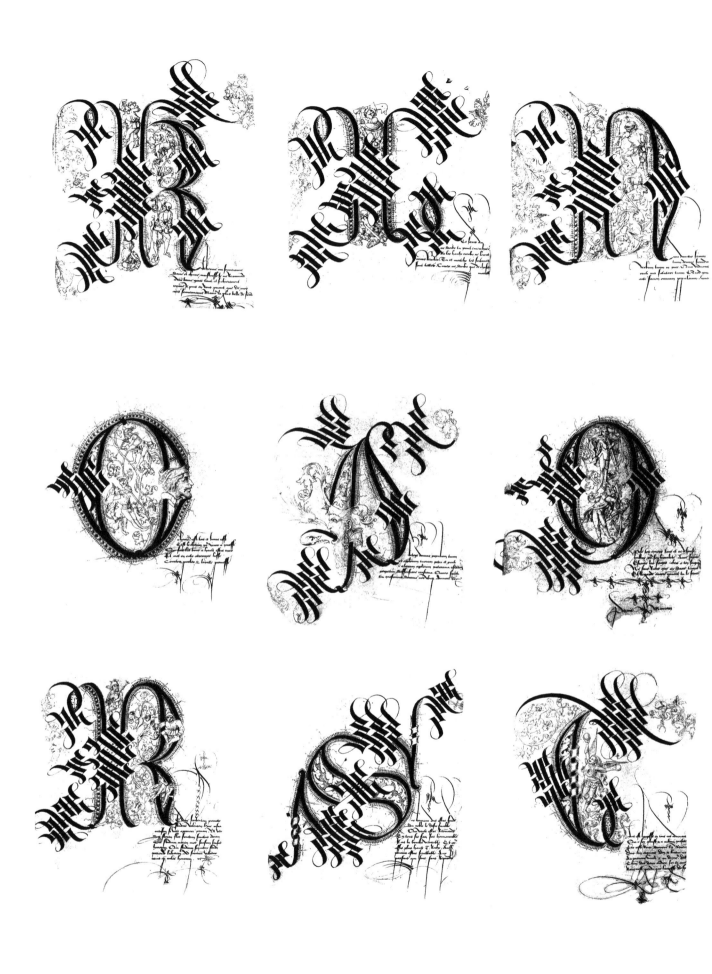

Gothic alphabet of Marie de Bourgogne, circa 1480.

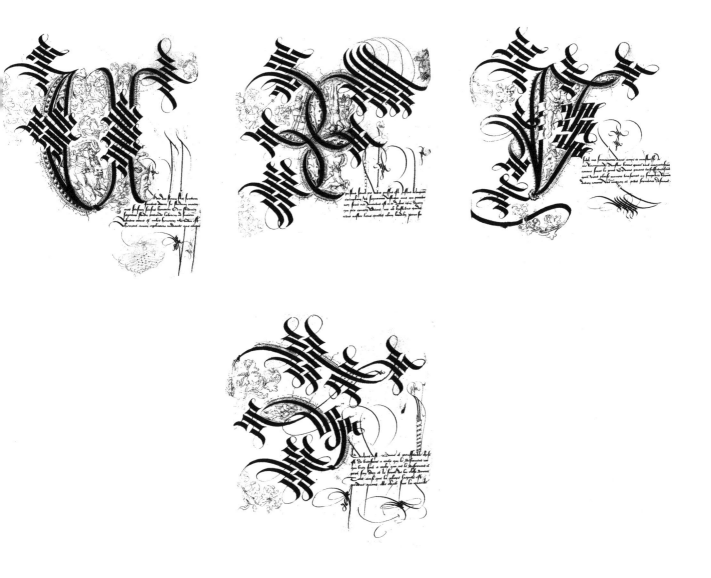

Gothic alphabet of Marie de Bourgogne, circa 1480.

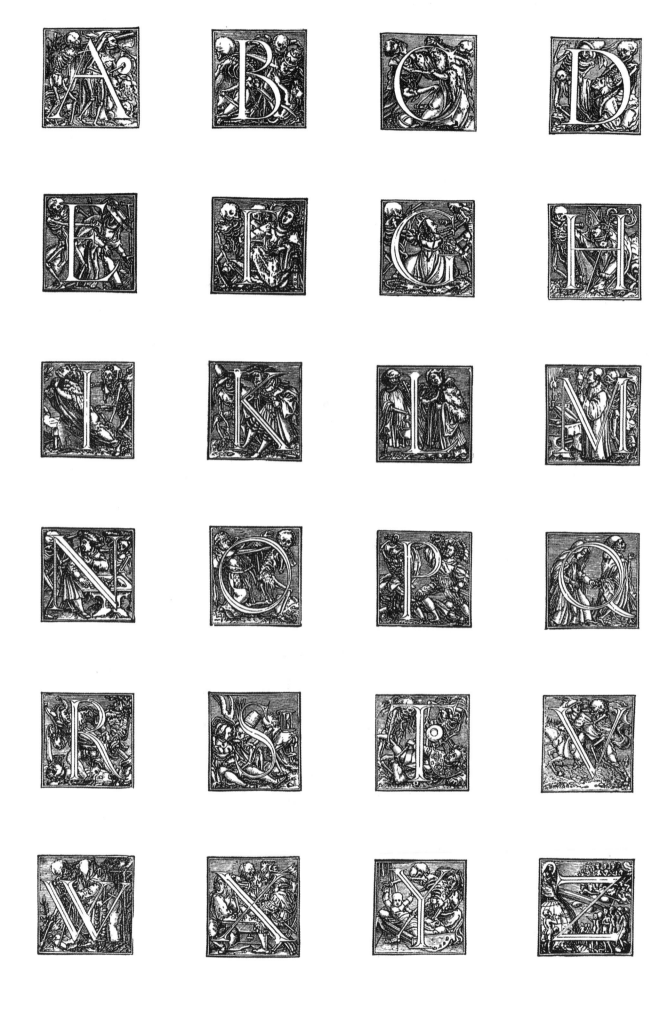

Hans Holbein. Alphabet of death, Dresden, sixteenth century.

P

Master E.S. Letter P, Germany, circa 1466-1467.

ANIMALS

... Lastly (I quote only one more of our dear Barnum's inventions from amongst twenty others), there appeared the following year a funny (comical) ABC priced at a penny piece, in which large letters painted in gaudy colours were depicted by pigs standing, lying, alive, dismembered, grouped, in the most grotesque positions and with naive or laughable verses by way of epigraphs. These animals having much physionomy, the draughtsman had succeeded in turning their ears, their corkscrew tails, their muzzles, to admirable effect...

(Hippolyte-Adolphe Taine. Vie et opinions de Monsieur Frédéric-Thomas Graindorge.)

Master E.S. Letters F and Q, Germany, circa 1466-1467.

Master E.S. Letter I, Germany, circa 1466-1467.

Alde. Letters decorated with animals, Venice, 1579.

26

Lucas Cranach. D. Aelt, Germany, 1534.

Anonymous. Animal alphabet, Netherlands, end of eighteenth century.

Animal alphabet, Paris, nineteenth century.

Ornamental capitals, France, seventeenth century.

Piranese, Ornamental capitals, Italy, eighteenth century.

Decorative alphabet in Chinese style, France, nineteenth century.

Decorative alphabet in Chinese style, France, nineteenth century.

33

Decorative alphabet in Chinese style, France, nineteenth century.

Initial from "Jugend", n°40, 1898.

FIGURES

... M is not only an introduction, a door with its two shutters divided by the cleft, our lips when they allow the breath to escape as in mute or in murmur (unless all those parallel vertical lines give us the impression of a forest), it is in the very interior of my own identity. Me, here I am, upstanding between my two walls, as in my home or in a chamber. I is a flaming torch. O is that mirror which is conscience; unless we prefer to see it as the core, or as that open window through which is communicated the internal light. The soul is me as a centre of aspiration;... Memory: I remember myself. I am a man or a woman, with my own mind, with an external face that is moulded on the internal. With a mask sometimes, a portable face attached to a handle...

(Paul Claudel. "Les mots ont une âme", in Positions et propositions, Œuvres en prose. © Éditions Gallimard, Paris.)

Jan Theodor de Bry. Nova alphati effictio/Nejw kunstlicher alphabet, Frankfurt, 1595.

Jan Theodor de Bry. Nova alphati effictio/Nejw kunstlicher alphabet, Frankfurt, 1595.

Jan Theodor de Bry. Nova alphati effictio/Nejw kunstlicher alphabet, Frankfurt, 1595.

Jan Theodor de Bry. Nova alphati effictio/Nejw kunstlicher alphabet, Frankfurt, 1595.

Jan Theodor de Bry. Nova alphati effictio/Nejw kunstlicher alphabet, Frankfurt, 1595.

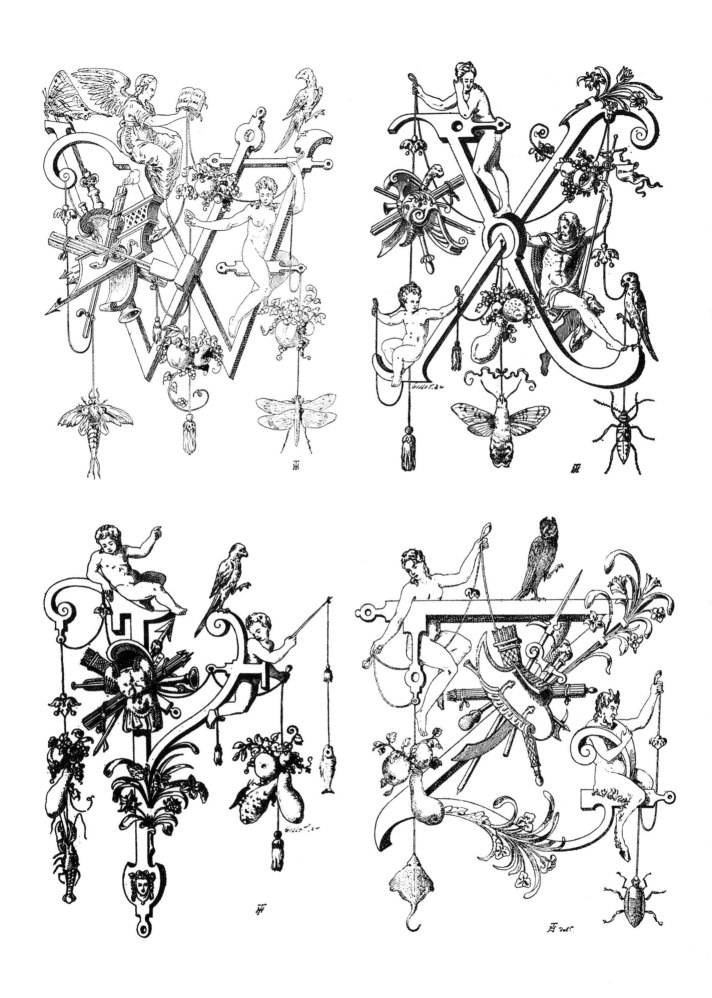

Jan Theodor de Bry. Nova alphati effictio/Nejw kunstlicher alphabet, Frankfurt, 1595.

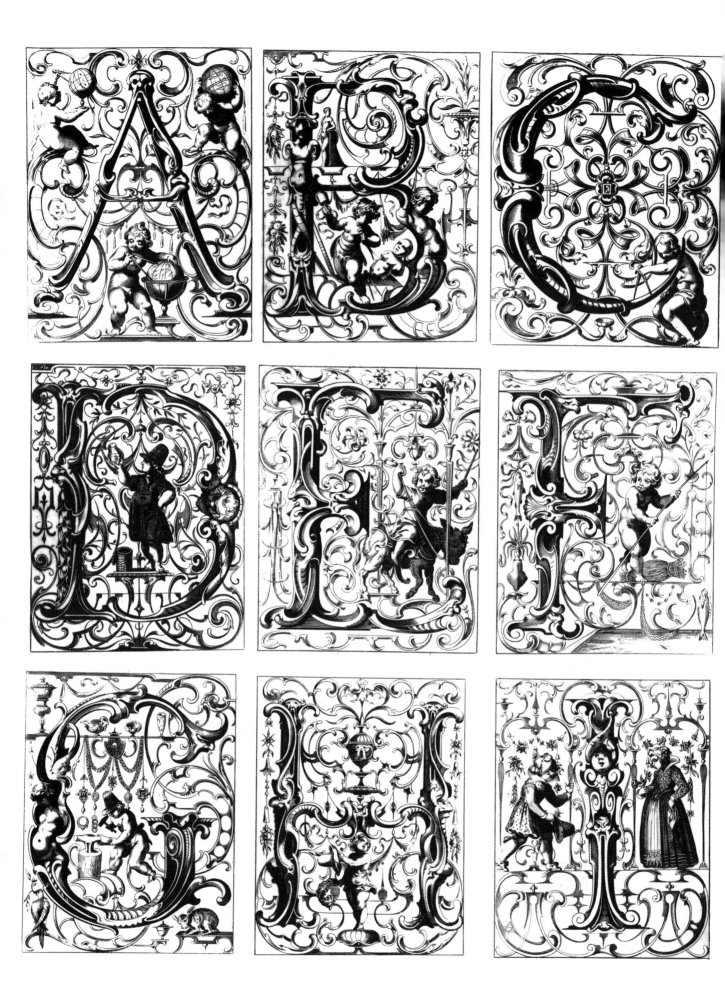

Lukas Killian. Newes/ABC/Buechlein inventirt, 1627.

44

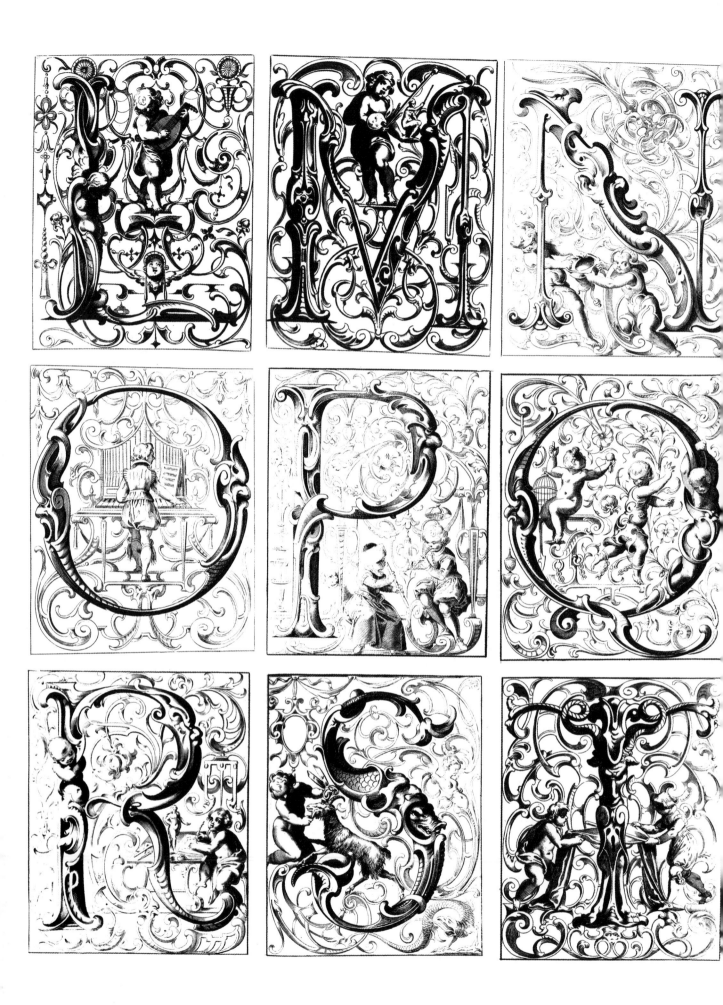

Lukas Killian. Newes/ABC/Buechlein inventirt, 1627.

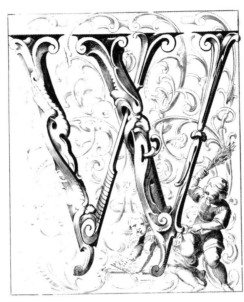

Lukas Killian. Newes/ABC/Buechlein inventirt, 1627.

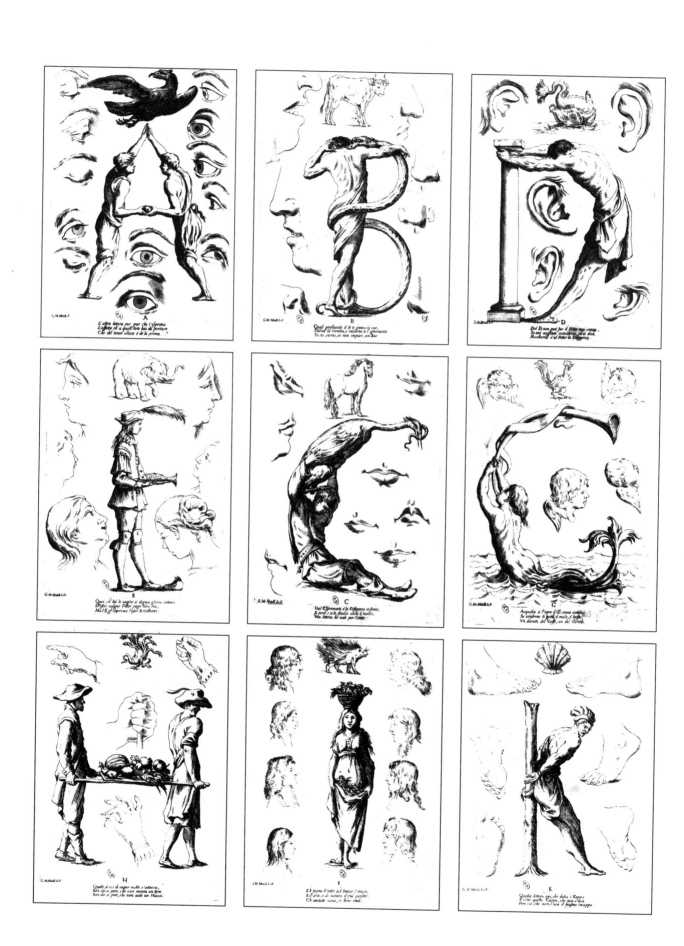

Giuseppe Mitelli. Dream alphabet, copy for drawing, Bologna, 1683.

F

Vuol' l'Esse dir Fatica, e senza alcuna
Difficolta da lei nasce souente
Vn second' esse, e questo è la Fortuna

Giuseppe Mitelli. Dream alphabet, copy for drawing, Bologna, 1683.

Giuseppe Mitelli. Dream alphabet, copy for drawing, Bologna, 1683.

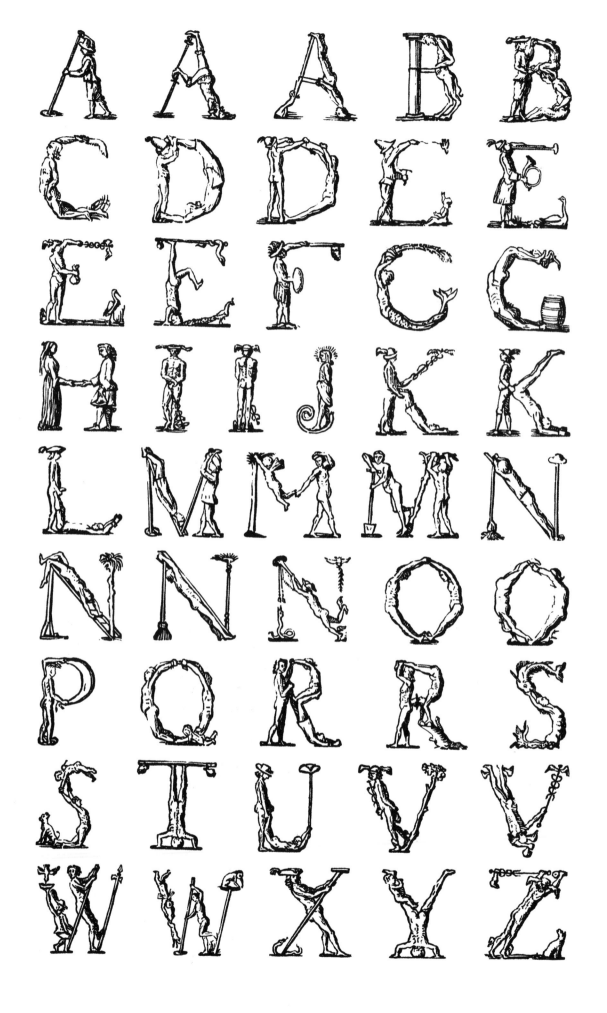

C.V. Noorde. Hieroglyphic alphabet, Netherlands, 1751.

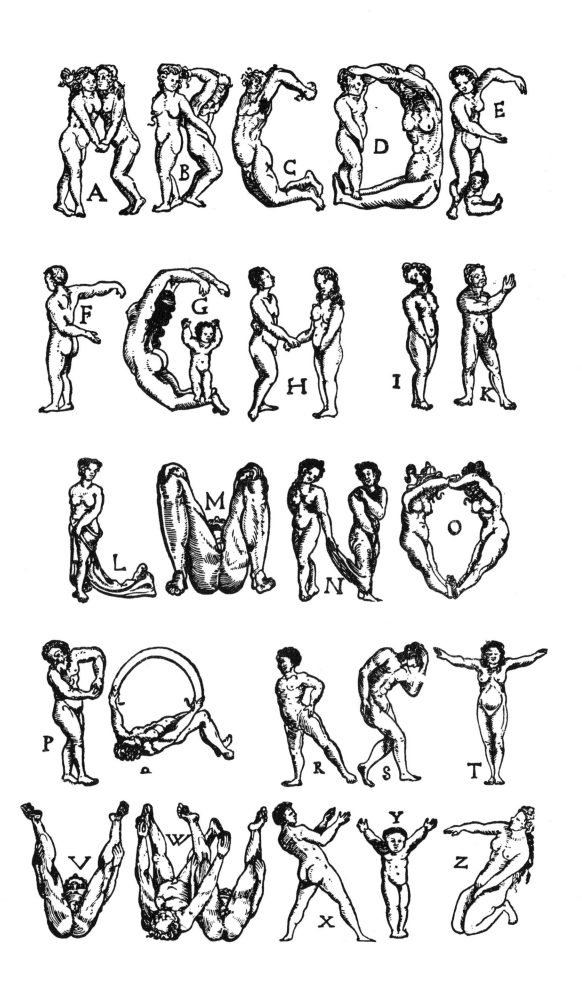

Peter Flötner. Menschenalphabet, Germany, circa 1534.

Holbein. Children's alphabet, Germany, sixteenth century.

Ornamental capitals, France, seventeenth century.

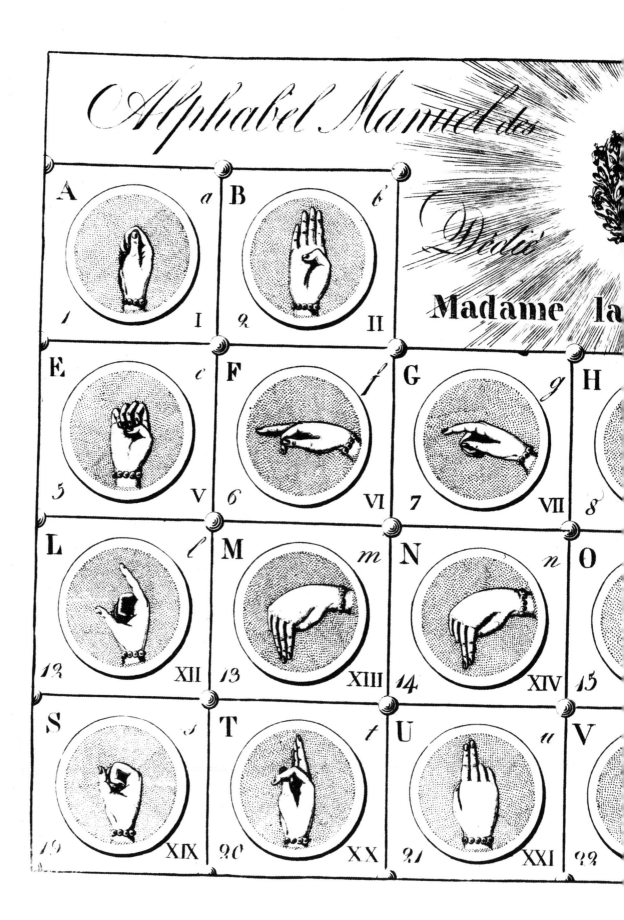

Manual alphabet of signs for the deaf and dumb, France, 1827.

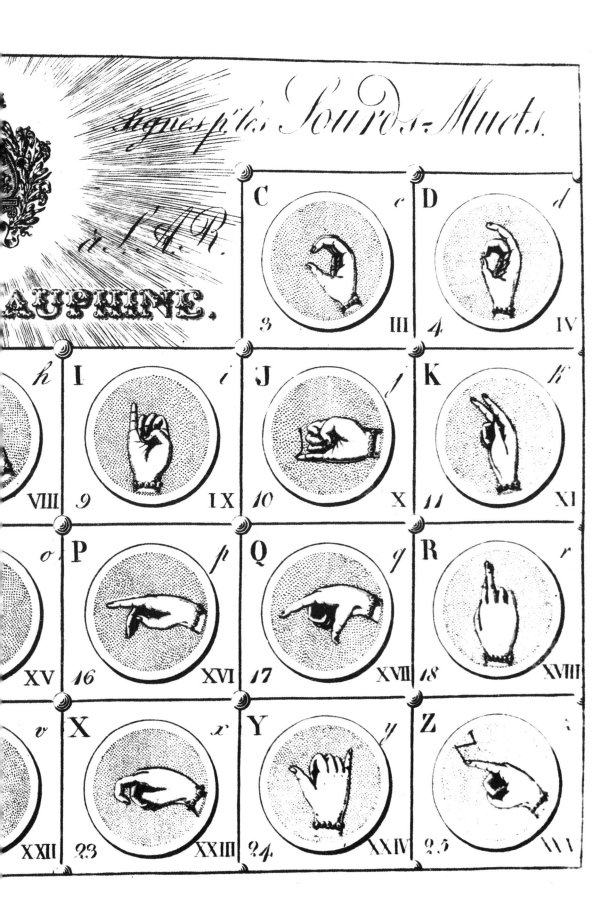

Signes p. les Sourds-Muets.

DAUPHINE.

Achille Devéria. Alphabet, France, nineteenth century.

Achille Devéria. Alphabet, France, nineteenth century.

Kuehtmann, Dresden, nineteenth century.

Kuehtmann, Dresden, nineteenth century.

Initials from "Jugend", n°40, 1898.

Initials from "Jugend", n°40, 1898.

Drawing competition in the creation of ornamental capitals, England, 1898.

Drawing competition in the creation of ornamental capitals, England, 1898.

LANDSCAPES

"The letters of the alphabet can be a beautiful thing, and yet they do not suffice to express sounds; as for sounds, we could not do without them, and yet they are greatly lacking in their capacity to express meaning, properly speaking; we attach importance to the letters and the sounds, and we have advanced no further than if we had nothing of all that; what we succeed in communicating, what may be transmitted to us, is never more than the most common part, and which is not worth the effort."

"You are avoiding my question", replied his friend, "for I do not see what relation that bears to the rocks and the ridges."

"If precisely I were to consider the clefts and crevices as letters, if I seek to decipher them, if I form words with them and if I learn to read them fluently, what objection could you make to that?"

"None, save that your alphabet appears to me to be somewhat oversized."

"Less than you believe; it must simply be learned, like any other. Nature has only one set of graphics, and here I do not have to lose myself in all sorts of scribblings. I do not have to fear that, as happens after bending for a long time, lovingly, over a manuscript, a rigorous critic may appear to assure me that it is all only a question of interpretation."

(Goethe. Wilhelm Meisters Wanderjahre oder Die Entsagenden.)

Piranese. Ornamental capitals, Italy, eighteenth century.

Piranese. Ornamental capitals, Italy, eighteenth century.

Ornamental capitals, Italy, eighteenth century.

Ornamental capital, France, seventeenth century.

A. Pazzi. Ornamental capitals, Italy, seventeenth century.

A. Pazzi. Ornamental capitals, Italy, seventeenth century.

Harmsen Co. Initials engraved in 1818, Netherlands.

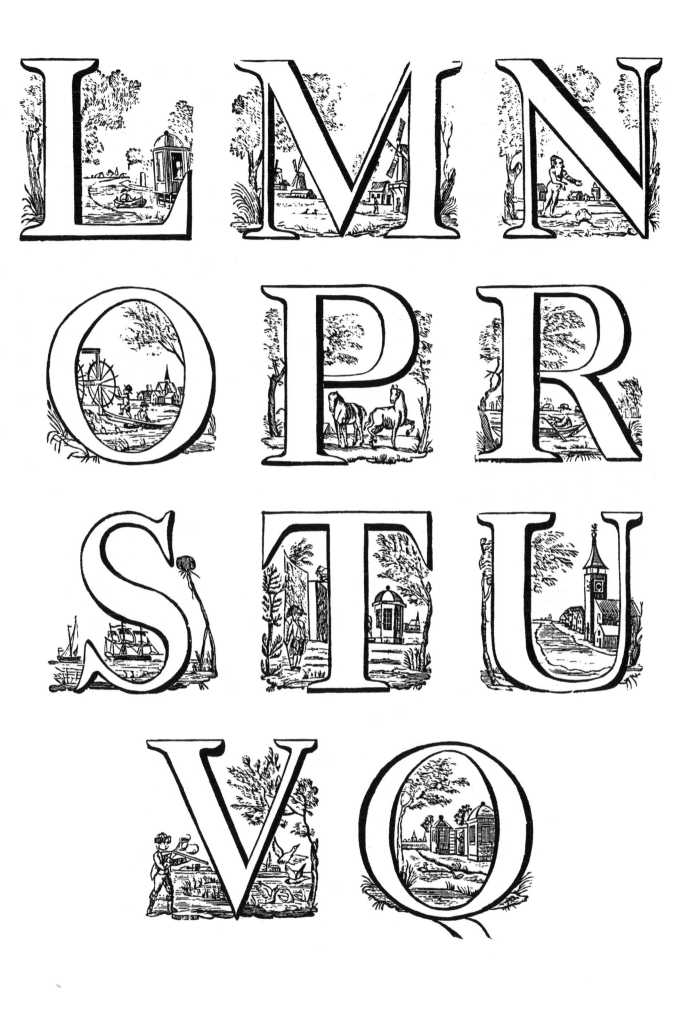

Harmsen Co. Initials engraved in 1818, Netherlands.

Harmsen Co Initials engraved in 1818, Netherlands

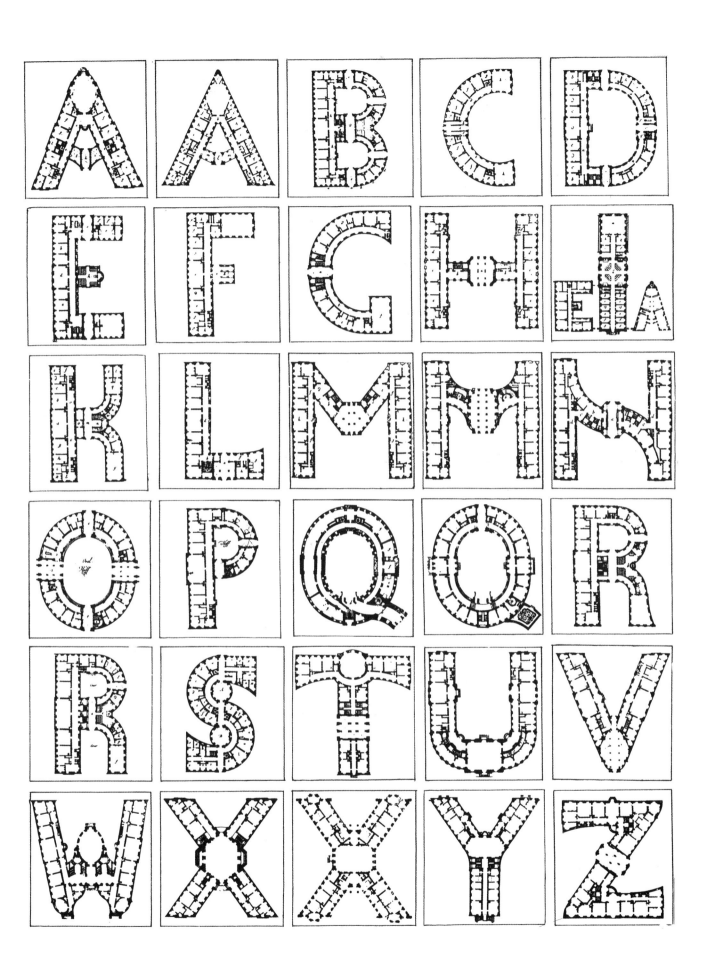

Johann David Steingruber. Architectonic alphabet, Swabach, 1773.

77

Drawing competition in ornamental capitals, Paris, 1899.

POPULAR IMAGERY

... His joy, his secret dream of devotion, was to live always in the company of a young being who would not grow up, whom he would instruct ceaselessly, through whose innocence he would love men. As of the third day he brought an alphabet. Muche enchanted him by his intelligence. He learnt his letters with that verve of Parisian street children. The images in the alphabet amused him extraordinarily... After two months, Muche was beginning to read fluently, and his copy-books were very clean.

(Emile Zola. Le ventre de Paris.)

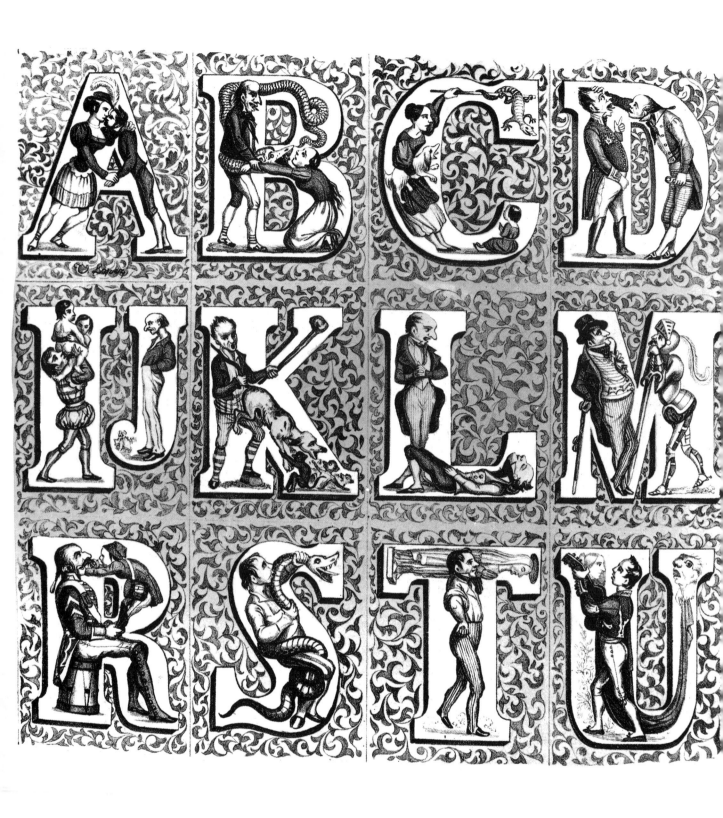

Comic alphabet, Paris, circa 1840.

Comic alphabet, Paris, circa 1840.

Daumier. Alphabet, Paris, 1836.

Daumier. Alphabet, Paris, 1836.

Ornamental capitals, France, nineteenth century.

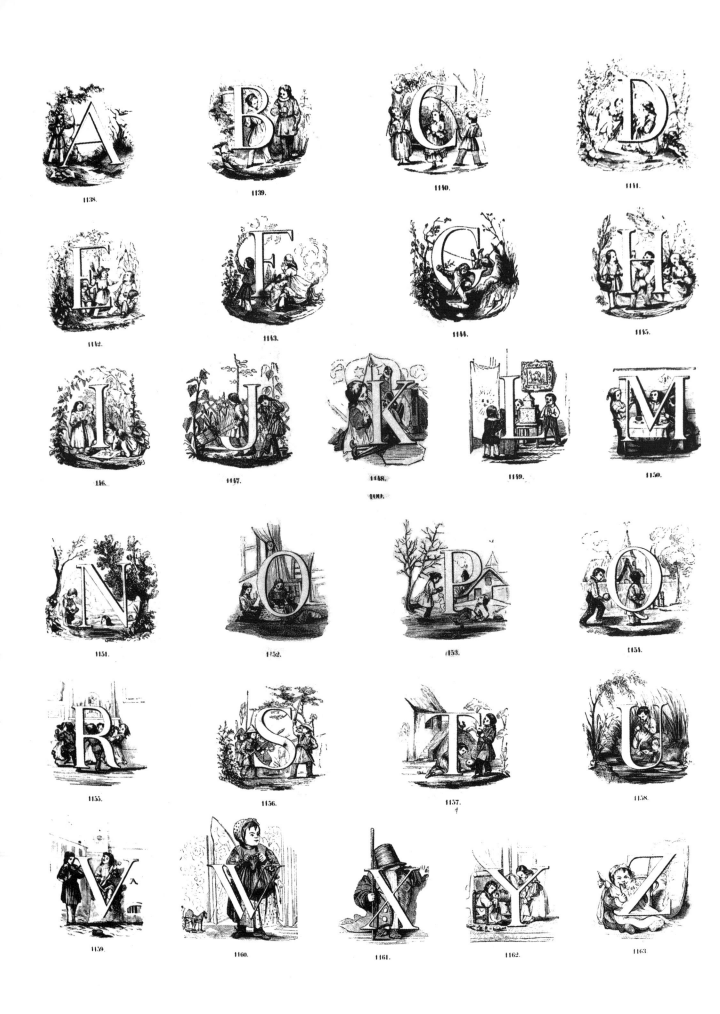

De Lacrampe et Cie printing-works. Children's alphabet, Paris, 1838.

Ch. Laboulaye. Specimens of letters from the Fonderie Générale, Paris, circa 1850.

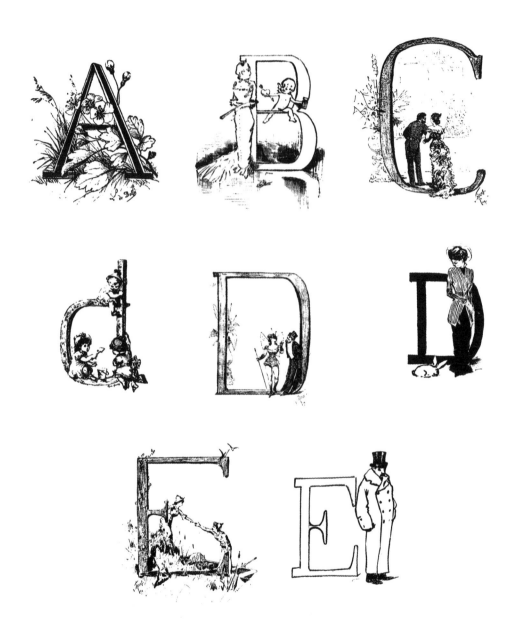

Arcos, Forain. Fantasy letters, Paris, nineteenth century.

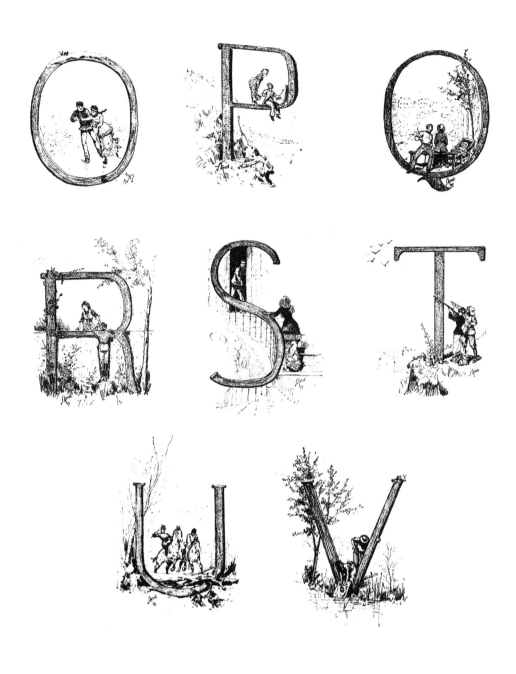

Arcos, Forain, Fantasy letters, Paris, nineteenth century.

Bibliography

Paul Claudel. *Les mots ont une âme, in Oeuvres en prose*, Paris, Bibliothèque de la Pléïade, Gallimard, 1965.
Gustave Flaubert. *La tentation de Saint Antoine*, Paris, 1874.
Goethe. *Wilhelm Meisters Wanderjahre oder Die Entsagenden.*
Victor Hugo. *France et Belgique. Alpes et Pyrénées. Voyages et excursions,* Paris, 1910.
Massin. *La lettre et l'image*, Paris, Gallimard, 1970.
Taine. *Vie et opinions de Monsieur Frédéric-Thomas Graindorge,* Paris, 1857.
Emile Zola. *Le ventre de Paris*, Paris, 1873.

PHOTOGRAPHIC CREDITS :

Bibliothèque des Arts Décoratifs - Paris - Collection Maciet pages 7-8-9-11-12-13-14-15-20-23-26-27-30-31-32-33-34-35-37-38-39-400-41-42-43-48-49-500-51-54-56-58-59-60-62-63-64-65-67-68-69-70-71-72-73-78-79-81-82-86-88-89-90-91. Bibliothèque des Arts Décoratifs - Paris pages 44-45-46-47. © Photo Réunion des Musées Nationaux, Musée du Louvre, collection Rothschild pages 16-17-18-19-21-24-25. © Photo Bibliothèque Nationale de France pages 8-9.

Achevé d'imprimer en mars 1995 par l'Imprimerie Hérissey
Nº d'imprimeur : 68392
Nº d'édition : 95 BK 13
Dépôt légal : 1er trimestre 1995
ISBN 2-87714-281-7

Imprimé en France